Table Of Contents

Corporations: Having A Third Form Of Family Credit, Making Your Financial Future A Reality, Using The Corporation To Protect Your Assets. Make Amazing Money Using Corporate Credit For Your Investment Accounts, Retirement Accounts, Education Accounts, and Financial Resources, Financing Business Goals, Entrepreneurs Starting a Business, Existing Businesses Looking to Expand, Merge or Change Availability of Credit.

Preface

First, let me tell you a little bit about myself. When I was in the seventh grade I was the kid selling candy out of my locker at school to make extra money. In the ninth grade that entrepreneurial spirit moved to selling other kids fireworks (not the safest way to make a buck but I had a product and people were buying). Later in life I moved up to a Real Estate License, trying to sell Nikken, Interior Design Nutritionals, selling loans, selling fire extinguishers, trying to invent, and many other endeavors that all were under-funded. To make a long story short I have tried 'just about everything'. Then I finally started getting smart. I went back to college and took some business classes, tried to read the books the rich were reading, learning about trusts, estate planning, the stock market, financial planning, business management, and more real estate books. All of this learning has become the basis for what I believe in life is the 'leg up' for anyone that isn't in their retirement years, doesn't have a lifetime of financial earnings to start any project they want, and has any type of entrepreneurial spirit or wants to start and/or continue building their own or their family's wealth goals. I hope this book provides one more tool in your arsenal that helps everyone achieve those goals.

When I first set out to learn about what a Corporation is and what it could do for my and later in life my family's goals, I didn't think that I would find so much information, so many companies just specializing in this field, and so many helpful people to guide my endeavors along the way. I am sure if let to ourselves without the nudge in the right direction (such as this book) and even without doing a little thinking outside the box, that we could all live our whole lives without the huge benefits that a corporation, our entrepreneurial spirit, and a little guidance have to offer.

It doesn't worry me that the average person reading this will know almost nothing about these tools. I believe that's what makes this book a great place to start learning from a resource that has devoted countless hours to reading book after book, then typing, then editing the forms and contracts available on the data disk. All this is intended so you can move on to your dreams instead of getting lost down every rabbit hole available without knowing the right direction to go in.

Please keep in mind (this is my disclaimer): Any information available here and on the data disk or roadmap are not intended as any type of advice and only intended as the best presentation of information that was and is available. If you need clarifications, seek advice, or want to learn more please, please don't be intimidated or averse to discussing <u>any</u> of your or your families business matters with certified and licensed attorneys, certified public accountants, certified financial planners, or any of the wonderful companies that are referred to throughout this text and data accompaniments. Thank You.

How This Booklet Can Help You and Your Family Along the Way:

- Extra Source Of Family Credit
- Protect Your Family's Assets
- Just-In-Case Funds
- Helping To Set Up IRA's, 529's, and Investment Accounts For Family Members (ie. Loans to the Family Pot Paid Off With Returns or Monthly Installments)
- Start A Business & Have the Best Source and Ease of Obtaining Financing/Credit Than Other Business Structures/Entity Structures (ie. Sole Proprietorships, LLC's, Partnerships all are more limited than and S-Corporation or Closed Corporation when it comes to obtaining credit and outside financing)
- Real Estate Investing
- If Your Business is in a Growth Phase You can use a Separate Corporation's Credit to give your business a Loan!!
- You can use a Corporation's Credit to Finance a Business Acquisition or Merger.

ACCOMPANYING THIS BOOK IS A ROADMAP WITH STEP BY STEP INSTRUCTIONS TO FORMING YOUR CORPORATION. PLEASE READ ALL OF THIS BOOK AND ENTREPRENEUR'S ULTIMATE GUIDE ON FORMING CORPORATIONS, LLC'S, SOLE PROPRIETORSHIPS, PARTNERSHIPS SO THAT YOU ARE BEST PREPARED TO USE THE CORPORATION AS A TOOL TO HELP YOUR GOALS BE ACHIEVED! GOOD LUCK IN ALL YOU DO!

ALSO IF YOU BOUGHT THE E-BOOK YOU MAY JUST COPY AND PASTE THE LINKS IN THIS BOOK INTO YOUR BROWSER, OR YOU CAN FIND ALL OF THESE LINKS ON THE WEB BY JUST TYPING THE LINKS OUT.

Student, Scholastic, Research Project, and Transition to Industry
As a student:
- You may be in the middle of your undergraduate studies
- You may be postgraduate working on a research project
- You may be postdoctoral even and working on any type of project or presentation to other schools or industry companies and personalities that your invention or research may present great opportunities to.
- You may be ready to start your own business and further research to add to the world's future.

Whether you are undergraduate or postgraduate working on paying for school (classes, units, books, gas, living expenses), or trying to find other sources of funding for your graduate project, research project, or transition to a business model that will either be accepted by industry or entrepreneurial in spirit, this opportunity to fund and fuel your goals and dreams is for you. By using a common business type (the Corporation) and a common financial gain strategy (the Investment: Mutual Funds or other type of portfolio), you can make any of your current goals that require financial input... a reality.

Almost all of our goals require a financial input or down payment until we can ACTUALLY profit from our hard work, ideas, and contributions to society. With a little help we can all move forward in this great age of opportunity even if the Financial Aid Department can approve us, or the Venture Capital World can fund 1% of ideas, or even if the NIH or the Government Grants Arena or any other Professionally Capable Funding Resources might not be Adequately capable of giving or providing or loaning or granting the means to <u>all</u> of our goals, this is a tool and a possibility that can and should and may aid what we all attempt to accomplish.

<u>Charitable Donations</u>

Currently only 30% of income for private foundations, charities, tax exempt charitable corporations, charitable trusts, and other groups that file taxes under the IRS 501(c)(3) tax exempt status may be derived from non-charitable support activities, or business activities that don't fall directly into the category of donations.

Using you corporation(s) activities and investments can greatly help support your donating capabilities and provide a perpetual gift in the form of annual investment returns that would otherwise be a one time gift. I am sure all of our families and communities would love to know you are creating perpetual gifts and giving instead of your one time annual gifts.

Instead of knowing you could only support one or two charities each year with one time gifts you could build your corporation's investment accounts over the years and gradually be able to do that much more in your lifetime.

Each of your normal annual gifts now becomes returns and giving for every year for the rest of your family's lifetimes and giving. This doesn't require having to set up a charity or deal with the intricacies of setting up charitable trusts as these types of formations can be difficult and are usually reserved for the more advanced financial planning scenarios. You can very simply set up your corporation and be going, giving, making a big difference from the day you start.

The corporation as a tool provides a great opportunity to advance your ability to be philanthropic and giving.

No matter what your goals, the main point is that having a corporation with its own credit, funds, and investments can pay all of its own fees, debt service, and provide income to make your other projects possible.

Inventors, Invention Groups, Researchers, Students, Professors, Research Fellows, Authors, Creators, and all Other Entrepreneurial Spirits:

Some conversations with venture capitalists reveal that many times as few as ONE OR TWO Percent of new ideas, and inventions are capitalized or are ever able to find any type of funding to become part of the market of new products. This reality is unfortunate and not the best model that we can hope for to make our dreams a reality. There are finally more tools and new ideas that can fill in the gaps that other sources of venture and funding aren't able.

If you are a part of an inventors group, why not have a corporation's credit invested to make sure your group can fund your ideas, startups, funding searches, research and development, product design, engineering design, facilities, equipment, labs, certifications, training, permits, application fees for the United States Patent and Trademark Organization, World Intellectual Property Organization, other funding application fees, and even lease and office equipment.

If you come up with good ideas all the time, why not find out how far they can go or make them real projects and products on you own.

COSTS will always exist, and new ones will come up!
Why not use a corporation and corporate credit investment returns to ensure YOU CAN FUND ANY GOALS for you, other inventors, other students, research, even as donations to help fund whole schools' projects and growth.

Don't wait NINE MONTHS TO ONE YEAR to find out your ideas are denied for funding.
Instructors and Fellows help your colleagues, students, research department, and teams secure funding: ANNUALLY! FOREVER!
Do you see new student ideas all the time, several times per semester, but you know the money isn't there or the NIH isn't funding that type of project at this time? I say the money IS THERE. Just as the banks have investment portfolios, charitable trusts have investment portfolios, private foundations, even other companies have their investments. This is all a normal part of financial planning and diversification that keeps profits and funding coming in. Your projects deserve to have access to this knowledge and the Corporation as a tool.

WHAT TO DO AND REMEMBER:

- Build Corporation (as per the steps outlined in the Corporation Formation Roadmap).
- Build Corporation Credit
- Don't Use More than 20% of the Corporations available credit so there will always be a great score and something else available.
- Invest in Mutual Funds with over 20% Returns per Year and Low Risk… This is an easy list to find: Morningstar.com and Create a Morningstar Profile/Login to gain best access to this free list capability. Also…Invest like a 20 Year Old. Account for the interest rate on credit lines and remember that your corporation is a perpetual person and don't invest like a ninny. Grow your means to supply your own financial help.
- Pay your taxes on annual returns.

- Account for your Debt Service for Corporate Credit Accounts MONTHLY (including the under 20% usage requirement of credit usage)
- Pay these bills monthly (if you follow the roadmap you will know how paypal can help you do this.
- You WILL have monthly debt service on revolving lines of credit or cards, until you get to the higher tiers to get signature credit… this is an advanced scenario… most of you won't see this option for several years unless you perfect your accounts attention.
- Pay for accounting, registered agent fees, annual reports, DNB fees, and state and IRS fees ANNUALLY
- WHAT IS LEFT IS WHAT YOU CAN USE FOR YOUR GOALS.
- $$$ FOR School, Books, Cash, Gas, Food, Lodging, DISPURSED TO YOU BY YOUR CORPORATION AS AN "ANNUAL PAYMENT FOR MANAGEMENT SERVICES" For Corporate Accounting and 1020 (IRS Corp Tax Form) and State Tax (Depends on the state you choose)
- Remember if you choose to incorporate in the state you will do business from then you must pay state fees, or you must pay foreign business fees if you incorporate in a state other than your state of locale or business dealings.

_____ 1)   First and Foremost: READ ENTREPRENEUR
MAGAZINE'S ULTIMATE BOOK ON FORMING:
CORPORATIONS, LLC'S SOLE PROPRIETORSHIPS, and
PARTNERSHIPS. This will be the BEST primer on what a
corporation is, what it can and can't do. Also the appendix will help
you see the benefits and drawbacks of incorporating in each state
along with contact information and websites.

_____ 2)   Choose a company from the list in this book to purchase your
aged corporation. If they don't have aged corporations from your
state you might search the Internet with [Aged Corporation your
state]. To start you should choose the state you live in until you
know more and are ready to possibly start your second corporation.
The company you choose will file your 'Articles of Incorporation' for
you with the Secretary of State. They will provide your transfer
documents for the corporation and copies of the Articles and other
documents filed with the Secretary of State. Some of the documents
you may receive copies of are 'Corporate Veil', 'Articles of
Incorporations', 'Statement of Incorporator', 'Statement of
Organization', and 'Receipt of Purchase'. State filing fees are a part
of the purchase price of an aged corporation.   ***Note: Issuing
Stock…When you are asked how you would like to issue your
corporations stock, the easiest start is giving the company selling you
your aged corporation the answer: "Between 1 to 500 shares at 0 par
value", when you are asked how you would like to have your stock
issued. Par Value = Stock Face Value. The lower number of shares

you are issued is best when your are learning about having your first corporation.

_____ 3)   You must have a registered agent. This means someone that receives mail and correspondence from the Secretary of State and forwards the mail to you. For a nominal transfer fee and $50.00/year Harvard Business Services is the best registered agent price in the industry. After you complete the purchase of your aged corporation you can give Harvard Business Services a call at: 800-345-2677 or online at http://www.delawareinc.com.

_____ 4)   Read Instructions for IRS Forms SS-4, IRS 1120, and IRS 2553 to familiarize yourself with the IRS rules regarding obtaining an Employer Identification Number, Taxes Your Corporation Will Pay, and how you define your corporation to the IRS, the State, Dun and Bradstreet, and other applications you fill out over time.

_____ 5)   Fill out and send in IRS Form SS-4 to obtain Your EIN or Employer Identification Number. This is your Tax ID Number.

_____ 6)   When you have obtained your EIN you will want to create a DUNS NUMBER with Dun & Bradstreet.

_____ 7)   Fill out and send in IRS form 2553 to define your corporation for the IRS, the State, and other applications. This form is your Election by a Small Business Corporation.

_____ 8)   Obtain and keep a printed copy of this years IRS form 1120 so that you will be ready at tax time.

_____ 9)   Obtain Certified Copies of the Documents that were filed with the Secretary of State for the state of your corporation.

_____ 10) Create a Bank Account With Certified Copies of State Filed Forms, Articles of Incorporation, EIN, Duns Number, Etc.

_____ 11) Make Sure if you are using your home for your business address that IRS, DNB, Your Bank, and other Creditors you work with know that is your status so there is no miscommunication and so no red flags or misinformation (intentional or unintentional) is interpreted!! [Home Based Business]

_____ 12) Set up a paypal account you will need the account and routing information from your business checking account. Set up your paypal account for [DONATIONS]

_____ 13) Set up a dedicated business email account.

_____ 14) Set up a dedicated business phone line with answering message or voicemail message with the name of your corporation mentioned. This helps all your interactions stay seen as professional as possible.

_____ 15) Category/Business Type: [OTHER] ON ALL APPLICATIONS. Later on you might find more specific needs and definitions for your first or later corporations when this happens you will choose the proper SIC Code for business type and make sure DNB, the IRS, Your Bank, and Any other creditor you work with is updated to your new SIC Code.

_____ 16) Dun & Bradstreet recognize a corporation can stand on its own at two to three years old. This is why you have purchased an aged corporation. Never use your Social Security Number and Your Credit on any applications for your corporation. Your business EIN and DUNS number is what you use for any credit.

_____ 17) Let Companies Incorporated (or another company listed in this book) set up your business credit and scores for $2500 ($1600 if you create your own DUNS Number and follow the instructions in this roadmap). They will ensure your Paydex Score is well over 80 (best corporate credit capability). Some people after using their service have secured anywhere from $100,000 to $400,000 in Corporate Credit!

_____ 18) Use your new credit to invest for returns, purchase a cabin or land and make a profit, or any number of the other uses you have read about in this book!

_____ 19) Revolving/ Secured Lines/ Installment Loans or Lines Paid Off. Looks Great

_____ 20) You are now well on your way, use the resources available here, and then when you are further down the road you can set up a second or third corporation for other projects and goals.

_____ 21) California: When doing business in California there are different rules than other states. The first time you pay yourself from your corporation, or any employee, more than $100 you must register with the EDD within fifteen days. This rule also applies to either paying a contractor or entering into any contract with a contractor for more than $600. You will also need to supply the EDD with other forms based on your formation situation and business goals. For a single Corporation officer/owner you would file forms DE6, DE7, and DE459 for reporting and exemptions. Please read the CA EDD Business owners manual to familiarize yourself with all the taxes and categorizations for your business for reporting and filing purposes.

_____ 22) California: If you form a Close Corporation instead of a standard Subchapter S-Corp you may have other reporting requirements with the FTB, or Franchise Tax Board, and/or even the Attorney Generals Office.

_____ 23) Other States: Please contact the right people to make sure all of your reporting requirements are handled appropriately with any and all state departments. Reporting may seem like a chore but these departments can be very helpful in helping you achieve your goals.

***HERE'S A VERY IMPORTANT NOTE:

IF YOU ARE PLANNING TO USE YOUR SINGLE CORPORATION FOR PROJECTS UNDER $500,000 YOU WILL BE USING (1) ONE CORPORATION AND BE USING THE SERVICES AVAILABLE FROM COMPANIES INCORPORATED, INC. IF YOU DECIDE ON LARGER PROJECTS AND TO USE THE PRODUCTS AND SERVICES AVAILABLE FROM AGED-CORPORATIONS.COM THEN YOU WILL HAVE TO FOLLOW THE INSTRUCTIONS AND ROADMAP ABOVE FOR EACH OF (3), (5), OR MORE CORPORATIONS. LARGER PROJECTS WILL REQUIRE THE USE OF SEVERAL CORPORATIONS DURING THE FIRST YEARS OF OWNERSHIP UNTIL YOUR CORPORATIONS CAN OBTAIN LARGER AMOUNTS OF CREDIT DOWN THE ROAD AND YOU CAN DISSOLVE EXTRA CORPORATIONS THAT YOU DO NOT NEED, OR UNTIL YOU HAVE PAID THE DEBT SERVICE OF CORPORATE CREDIT AND CAN DISSOLVE ADDITIONAL CORPORATIONS YOU OWN USING A LESSER NUMBER. EACH YEARS REPORTING AND ACCOUNTING AND TAXATION AND BINDER REQUIREMENTS WILL BE NECESSARY FOR EACH CORPORATION YOU OWN. IT WILL, HOWEVER, BE EASY TO MANAGE THIS IF YOU USE A GOOD PLANNER TO CALENDAR YOUR DUTIES.

Use the information and form on the next few pages to keep the right information and copies of documents in your Corporate Binder. Also you should use the list in this book titled: 'Corporate Binder Requirements' so that you have right right infomration about your corporation in one place. You must, by law, keep a corporate binder and your corporations' Articles, Bylaws, and Other docuements and annual minutes available for public

accessibility. While this may seem overkill the US government requires your Registered Agent, the Secretary of State and the Legal Location of the Corporation to have these documents available for verification.
Where To Find Forms:

IRS SS-4 (To Create Your EIN):

http://www.irs.gov/pub/irs-pdf/fss4.pdf
     (must have adobe acrobat)

IRS 2553 (To Define Your Business with the IRS):

http://www.irs.gov/pub/irs-pdf/f2553.pdf
     (must have adobe acrobat)

IRS 1120 (Your Annual Tax Form):

http://www.irs.gov/pub/irs-pdf/f1120.pdf
     (must have adobe acrobat)

CORPORATE BINDER REQUIREMENTS

A Sufficient Corporate Kit with Seal and Stock Pages Can Be Found At:
http://www.corpkit4less.com/items.cfm?catid=1

Corporate Binder Requirements:

Secretary Binder:
(Bylaws Part B(28))

Book of Minutes (all meetings)
- Time/Place of Holding
- Names of those present
- Number of Shares Present

Share Register
- Names/addresses of shareholders
- Number and classes of shares
- Number and date of share certificates issued and when
- Number and date of share certificates' cancellations
- Corporate Seal (kept in safe custody)
- Annual meeting of shareholders (minutes)
- Annual meeting of board (minutes)
- Compensation/Reimbursement of expenses of Director(s)/Officer(s)/Employee(s)/Otherwise
- Division of Corporations Certified Copies of Bylaws/Articles/Filings/Reports
- Federal 1120 (annual), 2553 (once), SS-4 (once)

CFO (Certified Financial Officer: You) Binder:
(Bylaws Part B(29))

Books and Records of Accounts of the properties and business transactions of the corporation including amounts of:
- Assets
- Liabilities
- Receipts
- Disbursements
- Gains
- Losses
- Capital
- Retained Earnings

- Shares

Current Bylaws Annual Meeting
      Elect Board
      Report Affairs of the Corporation
      Transact Other Business

***MANY OF THESE DOCUMENTS OR FORMS CAN BE FOUND
ONLINE:

NOLO.COM
LEGALZOOM.COM
ENTREPRENEURS ULTIMATE GUIDE TO FORMING
CORPORATIONS, LLC'S, PARTNERSHIPS, SOLE PROPRIETORSHIPS

CORPORATION INFORMATION TO KEEP TRACK OF IN YOUR BINDER

CORPORATION NAME:

_____

EIN Number:

_____

EFTPS (IRS PAYMENT SYSTEM)
PIN: _____
LOGIN: _____
PASSWORD: _____
EFTPS CONTACT PHONE#:_____

YOUR DEDICATED BUSINESS PHONE #: _____
YOUR DEDICATED BUSINESS EMAIL:
_____
YOUR WEBSITE INFORMATION:

_____

STATE REGISTERED IN: _____
CONTACT PH# FOR SECRETARY OF STATE: _____

REGISTERED AGENT INFORMATION:
Company Name:_____
Address: _____
Phone Number:

_____

Account Number: _____

DUNS NUMBER: _____
DUN & BRADSTREET LOGIN: _____
DUN & BRADSTREET PASSWORD:

_____

CONTACT PH # @ D & B:

_____

EXPERIAN SMALL BUSINESS CREDIT FILE INFORMATION:
EXPERIAN CREDIT FILE NUMBER:

_____

LOGIN:

_____

PASSWORD:

_____

CONTACT PH # @ EXPERIAN:

_____

BANKING INFORMATION:
BANK NAME FOR BUSINESS CHECKING:

_____

BANK CONTACT PH #:

_____

BANK ACCOUNT #:

_____

BANK ROUTING #:

_____

PIN NUMBER:

_____

MERCHANT ACCOUNT INFORMATION

NAME: _____
ACCOUNT #: _____
LOGIN: _____
PASSWORD: _____
PHONE #: _____

NAME: _____
ACCOUNT #: _____
LOGIN: _____
PASSWORD: _____
PHONE #: _____

NAME: _____
ACCOUNT #: _____
LOGIN: _____
PASSWORD: _____
PHONE #: _____

NAME: _____
ACCOUNT #: _____
LOGIN: _____

PASSWORD: _____

PHONE #: _____

SECURED CARDS INFORMATION:

NAME: _____

ACCOUNT #: _____

LOGIN: _____

PASSWORD: _____

PHONE #: _____

NAME: _____

ACCOUNT #: _____

LOGIN: _____

PASSWORD: _____

PHONE #: _____

NAME: _____

ACCOUNT #: _____

LOGIN: _____

PASSWORD: _____

PHONE #: _____

NAME: _____

ACCOUNT #: _____

LOGIN: _____

PASSWORD: _____

PHONE #: _____

SECRETARY BINDER FORMS:

Form 1

Secretary Binder: Share Register

Names and Addresses of Shareholders:

_____

(Name)
_____

(Address)
_____

(Name)
_____

(Address)
_____

(Name)
_____

(Address)
_____

(Name)
_____

(Address)
_____

(Name)
_____

(Address)
_____

(Name)
_____

(Address)

Number and Classes of Shares:

_____   _____

(Number)   (Class)
_____   _____

(Number)   (Class)

_____   _____
(Number)   (Class)

_____   _____
(Number)   (Class)

Number and Date of Share Certificates Issued:

_____   _____
(Number)   (Date)

_____   _____
(Number)   (Date)

_____   _____
(Number)   (Date)

_____   _____
(Number)   (Date)

_____   _____
(Number)   (Date)

_____   _____
(Number)   (Date)

_____   _____
(Number)   (Date)

Number and Date of Share Certificates' Cancellations:

_____   _____
(Number)   (Date)

_____   _____
(Number)   (Date)

_____   _____
(Number)   (Date)

_____   _____
(Number)   (Date)

_____   _____
(Number)   (Date)

_____   _____
(Number)   (Date)

_____   _____
(Number)   (Date)

Form 2

Secretary Binder   Compensation and Reimbursement of Expenses of
Directors, Officers, Employees, Other

_____

(Name)

_____ Director / Officer / Employee /

Other₁

(Position)

If 'Other₁' Please Explain Position or 'Contractor':

_____

_____ Compensation / Reimbursement

(Amount)

_____

(Name)

_____ Director / Officer / Employee /

Other₁

(Position)

If 'Other₁' Please Explain Position or 'Contractor':

_____

_____ Compensation / Reimbursement

(Amount)

_____

(Name)

_____ Director / Officer / Employee /

Other₁

(Position)

If 'Other₁' Please Explain Position or 'Contractor':

_____

_____ Compensation / Reimbursement

(Amount)

_____

(Name)

_____ Director / Officer / Employee /

Other₁

(Position)

If 'Other₁' Please Explain Position or 'Contractor':

_____

_____ Compensation / Reimbursement
(Amount)

_____
(Name)
_____ Director / Officer / Employee /
Other₁
(Position)
If 'Other₁' Please Explain Position or 'Contractor':

_____
_____ Compensation / Reimbursement
(Amount)

_____
(Name)
_____ Director / Officer / Employee /
Other₁
(Position)
If 'Other₁' Please Explain Position or 'Contractor':

_____
_____ Compensation / Reimbursement
(Amount)

_____
(Name)
_____ Director / Officer / Employee /
Other₁
(Position)
If 'Other₁' Please Explain Position or 'Contractor':

_____
_____ Compensation / Reimbursement
(Amount)

_____
(Name)
_____ Director / Officer / Employee /
Other₁
(Position)
If 'Other₁' Please Explain Position or 'Contractor':

_____
_____ Compensation / Reimbursement
(Amount)

Form 3

Secretary Binder: Book of Minutes   Annual Meeting of
Shareholders

<u>Time and Place of Holding:</u>

_____ AM / PM

_____
(Time)   (Building and Address)

_____
(Place: Building and Address cont.)

<u>Names of Those Present:</u>

_____
_____
_____
_____
_____
_____
_____
_____
_____
_____
_____
_____
_____

<u>Number of Shares Present:</u>

_____Shares

<u>Minutes:</u>

[Once for every meeting]

Form 4

Secretary Binder: Book of Minutes   Annual Meeting of Board

Time and Place of Holding:

_____ AM / PM

_____
(Time)   (Building and Address)

_____
(Place: Building and Address cont.)

Names of Those Present:

_____
_____
_____
_____
_____
_____
_____
_____
_____
_____
_____
_____
_____
_____

Number of Shares Present:

_____Shares

Minutes:

[Once for every meeting]

Form 5

Secretary Binder: Book of Minutes

<u>Time and Place of Holding:</u>

_____ AM / PM
     _____
(Time)   (Building and Address)

_____
(Place: Building and Address cont.)

<u>Names of Those Present:</u>

_____
_____
_____
_____
_____
_____
_____
_____
_____
_____
_____
_____
_____

<u>Number of Shares Present:</u>

_____ Shares

<u>Minutes:</u>

[Once for every meeting]

BUSINESS PLAN PARTS: This list should serve as a guide if you are going to use this book and your corporation for a business endeavor, or, you may use a regular business plan along with your home accounting and/or excel to help develop and chart your plans, then you can update your business plan as you go and track your successes.

A Business Plan Contains:

1.0 Executive Summary
      1.1 Objectives
      1.2 Mission
      1.3 Keys to Success
2.0 Company Summary
      2.1 Company Ownership
      2.2 Start-Up Summary
      2.3 Company Locations and Facilities
3.0 Products
      3.1 Competitive Comparison
      3.2 Future Products
4.0 Market Analysis and Summary
      4.1 Market Segmentation
      4.2 Market Needs
      4.3 Competition and Buying Patterns
5.0 Strategy and Implementation Summary
      5.1 Competitive Edge
      5.2 Sales Forecast
6.0 Management Summary
7.0 Financial Plan
      7.1 Important Assumptions
      7.2 Key Financial Indicators
      7.3 Break-Even Analysis
      7.4 Projected Profit and Loss
      7.5 Projected Cash Flow
      7.6 Projected Balance Sheet

*Note: Some parts of a standard business plan may not apply to all business types and family corporation use.

Recommended Reading

Entrepreneur Magazine's Guide To Forming Corporations, LLC's,
Partnerships, Sole Proprietorships
NOLO: Learn About Law Series
The Trust Workbook
The Equity Sharing Manual
52 Homes in 52 Weeks
Tenancy In Common (D. Andy Sirkin)
Inventors Book: Docie Inventor's Bible

****Best Price Corporate Binder and Seal Kit

From $23
http://www.corpkit4less.com/items.cfm?catid=1

Companies That Sell Aged Corporations and Help Build Corporate Credit:

Corporations Today, Inc
1712 Pioneer Ave Second Floor Suite 200
Cheyenne, WY 82001
800-632 3757
307-632-1800 (Outside US)
307-632-3886 (Fax)
www.corporationstoday.com
info@corporationstoday.com

Silver State Business Builders
9061 W. Sahara Avenue
Las Vegas, NV 89117
877-799-2677
702-795-8200
702-248-6194 (fax)
http://www.fastestbusinesscredit.com

Companies Incorporated
28015 Smyth Drive
Santa Clarita, CA 91355
800-830-1055
661-253-3303 (International)
http://www.companiesinc.com

Locations:

Las Vegas, Nevada Address:
Companies Incorporated
3540 W Sahara Avenue #202
Las Vegas NV 89102

Carson City, Nevada Office:
Companies Incorporated
1802 N Carson Street Suite 212
Carson City NV 89701

Wilmington, Delaware Address:

Companies Incorporated
1201 Orange Street #600
Wilmington DE 19801
Wholesale Shelf Corporations
228 Park Avenue South
New York, NY 10003
800-846-2001
866-949-9081
http://www.wholesaleshelfcorporations.com

Seasoned Corporations
The Colony
Texas, 75056
972-937-7225
http://www.seasonedcorporations.com/contact.htm

Business Credit Magic
200 South Virginia Street, 8th Floor
Reno, NV 89501
800-616-8007
http://www.businesscreditmagic.com

Laughlin Associates
2533 N. Carson Street
Carson City, Nevada 89706
888-273-8152
775-883-8484
775-883-4874
http://www.laughlinusa.com

Nevada Corporate Office
3161 S. Rainbow Blvd.
Las Vegas, NV 89113
702-448-1414
646-349-3978 (fax)
http://nevadacorporateoffice.com

The Company Corporation
2711 Centerville Road, Suite 400
Wilmington, DE 19808
800-818-6082
302-636-5440 (International)

302-636-5454 (fax)
http://www.incorporate.com

Harvard Business Services
16192 Coastal Highway
Lewes, DE 19958
800-345-2677
302-645-7400
302-645-1280
http://www.delawareinc.com/aboutus

****Advanced Projects and Higher Amounts of Corporate Credit Building

Aged-Corporations.com
3780 Old Norcross Road
Bldg 103, Suite 324
Atlanta, GA 30096
877-721-2677

NOTES AND TO DO LISTS

NOTES AND TO DO LISTS

Just to finish off this introductory book I have included a copy of the Bylaws that are available from Entrepreneurs Guide to Forming Corporation, LLC's, Partnerships, Sole Proprietorships. The reason for including this document here is that you will need one to be the guidelines, or rules, that your corporation will follow. Reading and eventually using this copy (mainly reading for starters) is to familiarize yourself with the intricacies of the Corporation as a separate entity. You must create and have Bylaws and Articles of Incorporation. Many of the steps to formation will require certified copies from your state of incorporation in order to establish accounts and credibility. Please don't be afraid of how complex all of this is. It does take work and learning and time and effort. You are capable of all of these with a little patience and sometimes the humility to ask qualified professionals in your town the questions to learn more.

BYLAWS OF [CORPORATION NAME]

Part A. Board of Directors

1. Subject to state law and the articles of incorporation, the business and affairs of this corporation shall be managed by and all corporate powers shall be exercised by or under the direction of the board of directors.

2. Each director shall exercise such powers and otherwise perform such duties in good faith, and in the manner provided for by law.

3. This corporation shall have [INSERT THE NUMBER OF DIRECTORS] directors. This number may be changed by amendment of the bylaws, adopted by the vote or written consent of a majority of shareholders entitled to vote. The term "board of directors" as used in these bylaws means the number of directors authorized in this paragraph, even if that number is one.

4. Directors shall be elected at each annual meeting of the shareholders to hold office until the next annual meeting, subject to any rights of shareholders outlined in any shareholders' agreement. Each director, including a director elected to fill a vacancy, shall hold office until

expiration of the term for which elected and until a successor has been elected and qualified.

5. Vacancies in the board of directors may be filled by a majority of the remaining directors, though less than a quorum, or by a sole remaining director. Each director so elected shall hold office until the next annual meeting of shareholders and until a successor has been elected and qualified.

6. A vacancy in the board of directors shall be deemed to exist in the event of the death, resignation, or removal of any director, or if the shareholders fail, at any meeting of the shareholders at which any directors are elected, to elect the full number of authorized directors. The shareholders may elect a director or directors to fill any vacancy or vacancies not filled by the directors, by any such election by written consent shall require a consent of a majority of the outstanding shares entitled to vote. Any director may resign effective upon giving written notice to the President, or the Secretary, unless the notice specifies a later time for that resignation to become effective. If the resignation of a director is effective at a future time, the shareholders may elect a successor to take office when the resignation becomes effective. No reduction of the authorized number of directors shall have the effect of removing any director before the director's term of office expires.

7. The entire board of directors or any individual director named may be removed from office as provided by state law. In such a case the shareholder(s) may elect a successor director to fill such vacancy for the remaining unexpired term of the director so removed.

8. Regular meetings of the board of directors shall be held at any place within or without the state that has been designated from time to time by resolution of the board. In the absence of such resolution, regular meetings shall be held at the principal executive office of the corporation. Special meetings of the board shall be held at any place within or without the state that has been designated in the notice of the meeting, or, if not stated in the notice or there is no notice, at the principal executive office of the corporation. Any meeting, regular or special, may be held by a conference telephone or similar communication equipment, so long as all directors participating in such meeting can hear one another, and all such directors shall be deemed to have been present in person at such meeting.

9. Immediately following each annual meeting of shareholders, the board of directors shall hold a regular meeting for the purpose of organization, the election of officers, and the transaction of other business. Notice of this meeting shall not be required. Minutes of any meeting of the board, or any committee of the board, shall be maintained by the Secretary or other officer designated for that purpose.

10. Other regular meetings of the board of directors shall be held without call at such time as shall from time to time be fixed by the board of directors. Such regular meetings may be held without notice, provided the time and place of such meetings has been fixed by the board of directors, and further provided the notice of any change in the time of such meeting shall be given to all the directors. Notice of a change in the determination of the time shall be given to each director in the same manner as notice for special meetings of the board of directors. If said day falls upon a holiday, such meetings shall be held on the next succeeding day thereafter.

11. Special meeting of the board of directors for any purpose or purposes may be called at any time by the Chairman of the board or the President or any Vice President or the Secretary or any two directors.

12. Notice of the time and place for special meetings shall be delivered personally or by telephone to each director or sent by first-class mail or telegram, charges prepaid, addressed to each director at his or her address as it is shown in the records of the corporation. In case such notice is mailed, it shall be deposited in the United Stats mail at least ten (10) days prior to the time of holding of the meeting. In case such notice is delivered personally, or by telephone or telegram, it shall be delivered personally, or by telephone or to the telegram company at least forty-eight (48) hours prior to the time of the holding of the meeting. Any oral notice given personally or by telephone may be communicated to either the director or to a person at the office of the director who the person giving the notice has reason to believe will promptly communicate such notice to the director. The notice need not specify the purpose of the meeting, nor the place, if the meeting is to be held at the principal executive office of the corporation.

13. The transactions of any meeting of the board of directors, however called, noticed, or wherever held, shall be as valid as though had at a meeting duly held after the regular call and notice if a quorum be

present and if, either before or after the meeting, each of the directors not present signs a written waiver of notice, a consent to holding the meeting, or an approval of the minutes thereof. Waiver of notices or consents need not specify the purpose of the meeting. All such waivers, consents, and approvals shall be filed with the corporate records or made part of the minutes of the meeting. Notice of a meeting shall also be deemed given to any director who attends the meeting without protesting, prior thereto or at its commencement, the lack of notice to such director. A majority of the authorized number of directors shall constitute a quorum for the transaction of business, except to adjourn as otherwise provided in these bylaws. Every act or decision done or made by a majority of the directors present at a meeting duly held at which a quorum was present shall be regarded as the act of the board of directors.

14. A majority of the directors present, whether or not constituting a quorum, may adjourn any meeting to another time and place.

15. Notice of the time and pace of the holding of an adjourned meeting need not be given, unless the meeting is adjourned for more than twenty-four (24) hours, in which case notice of such time and place shall be given prior to the time of the adjourned meeting to the directors who were not present at the time of the adjournment.

16. Any action required or permitted to be taken by the board of directors may be taken given a meeting with the same force and effect as if taken by unanimous vote of directors, if authorized by a writing signed individually or collectively by all members of the board. Such consent shall be filed with regular minutes of the board.

17. Directors and members of a directors' committee may receive such compensation and such reimbursement of expenses, as may be fixed or determined by resolution of the board of directors. Nothing herein contained shall be construed to preclude any director from serving the corporation in any other capacity as an officer, employee, or otherwise, and receiving compensation for such services.

18. Committees of the board may be appointed by resolution passed by a majority of the whole board. Committees shall be composed of two (2) or more members of the board and shall have such powers of the board as may be expressly delegated to them by resolution of the board of directors. The board may designate one (1) or more

directors as alternate members of any committee, who may replace any absent member at any meeting of the committee. Committees shall have such powers of the board of directors as may be expressly delegated to them by resolution of the board of directors.

19. The board of directors from time to time may elect one (1) or more persons to be advisory directors, who shall not by such appointment be members of the board of directors. Advisory directors shall be available from time to time to perform special assignments specified by the President, to attend meetings of the board of directors upon invitation, and to furnish consultation to the board. The period during which the title shall be held may be prescribed by the board of directors. If no period is prescribed, title shall be held at the pleasure of the board.

Part B. Officers

20. The principal officers of the corporation shall be a President, a Secretary, and a Chief Financial Officer who may also be called Treasurer. The corporation may also have, at the discretion of the board of directors, one or more Vice Presidents, one or more Assistant Secretaries, and such other officers as may be appointed in accordance with paragraph 22 of these bylaws. One person may hold two or more offices.

21. The principal officers of the corporation, except such officers as may be appointed in accordance with paragraph 22 of these bylaws, shall be chosen by the board of directors, and each shall serve at the pleasure of the board of directors, subject to the rights, if any, of an officer under any contract of employment

22. The board of directors may empower the President to appoint and remove such officers (other than the principal officers) as the business of the corporation may require, each of whom shall hold office for such period, have such authority and perform such duties as are provided in the bylaws or as the board of directors may from time to time determine.

23. Subject to the rights, if any, of an officer under any contract of employment, any officer may be removed, either with or without cause, by a majority of the directors at that time in office, at any regular or special meeting of the board, or, excepting the case of an

officer chosen by the board of directors, by any officer upon whom such power of removal may be conferred by the board of directors.

24. A vacancy in any office because of death, resignation, removal, disqualification, or any other cause shall be filled in the manner prescribed in these bylaws for regular appointments to such office.

25. The Chairman of the board, if an officer be elected, shall, if present, preside at all meetings of the board of directors and exercise and perform such other powers and duties as may from time to time be assigned to him by the board of directors or prescribed by the bylaws. If there is no President, the Chairman of the board shall in addition be the Chief Executive Officer of the corporation and shall have the powers and duties prescribed in paragraph 26 of these bylaws.

26. Subject to such supervisory powers, if any, as may be given by the board of directors to the Chairman of the board, if there be such an officer, the President shall be the Chief Executive Officer of the corporation and shall, subject to the control of the board of directors, have general supervision, direction, and control of the business and the officers of the corporation. He or she shall preside at all the meetings of shareholders and, in absence of the Chairman of the board, or if there be none, at all meetings of the board of directors. He or she shall have the general powers and duties of management usually vested in the office of President of a corporation, shall be ex officio a member of all the standing committees, including the executive committee, if any, and shall have such other powers and duties as may be described by the board of directors or the bylaws.

27. In the absence or disability of the President, the Vice Presidents, if any, in order of their rank as fixed by the board of directors, shall perform all the duties of the President, and so acting shall have all the powers of, and be subject to the restriction upon, the President. The Vice Presidents shall have such other powers and perform such other duties as from time to time may be prescribed for them respectively by the board of directors or the bylaws, the President, or the Chairman of the board.

28. The Secretary shall keep or cause to be kept at the principal executive office or such other place as the board of directors may order, a book of minutes of all meetings of directors, committees of directors, and shareholders, with the time and place of holding, whether regular or

special, and, if special, how authorized, the notice thereof given, the names of those present at directors' and committee meetings, the number of shares present or represented at shareholders' meetings, and the proceedings thereof. The Secretary shall keep or cause to be kept at the principal office or at the office of the corporation's transfer agent, a share register, or duplicate share register, showing the names of the shareholders and their addresses; the number and classes of shares held by each; the number and date of certificates issued for the same; and the number and date of cancellation of every certificate surrendered for cancellation. The Secretary shall give or cause to be given notice of all meetings of the shareholders and of the board of directors required by the bylaws or bylaw of all meetings of the shareholders an d of the board of directors required by the bylaws or bylaw of all meetings of the shareholders and of the board of directors required by the bylaws or bylaw to be given, shall keep the seal of the corporation in safe custody, and shall have such other powers and perform such other duties as may be prescribed by the board of directors or by the bylaws.

29. The Chief Financial Officer shall keep an d maintain, or cause to be kept and maintained, adequate and correct books an d records of accounts of the properties and business transactions of the corporation, including accounts of its assets, liabilities, receipts, disbursements, gains, losses, capital, retained earnings, and shares. The books of account shall at all reasonable times be open to inspection by any director. The Chief Financial Officer shall deposit all moneys and other valuables in the name and to the credit of the corporation with such depositories as may be designated by the board of directors. He or she shall disburse the funds of the corporation as may be ordered by the board of directors, shall render to the President and directors, whenever they request it, an account of all of his or her transactions as Chief Financial Officer and of the financial condition of the corporation, and shall have other powers and perform such other duties as may be prescribed by the board of directors or the bylaws.

Part C. Shareholders

30. Meetings of shareholders shall be held at any place designated by the board of directors. In the absence of any such designation, shareholders' meetings shall be held at the principal executive office of the corporation.

31. The annual meeting of the shareholders shall be held on March 1. If this day be a legal holiday, then the meeting shall be held on the next succeeding business day, at the same time. At the annual meeting, the shareholders shall elect a board of directors, report the affairs of the corporation, and transact such other business as may properly be brought before the meeting. If the above date is inconvenient, the annual meeting of shareholders shall be held each year on a date and at a time designated by the board of directors within twenty (20) days of the above date upon proper notice to all shareholders.

32. A special meeting of the shareholders, for any purpose or purposes whatsoever, may be called at any time by the board of directors, or by the Chairman of the board of directors, or by the President, or by one or more shareholders holding shares in the aggregate entitled to cast not less than 10% of the votes at any such meeting. If a special meeting is called by any person or persons other than the board of directors, the request shall be in writing, specifying the time of such meeting and the general nature of the business proposed to be transacted, and shall be delivered personally or sent by registered mail or by telegraphic or other facsimile transmission to the Chairman of the board, the President, any Vice President, or the Secretary of the Corporation. The officer receiving such request shall forthwith cause notice to be given to the shareholders entitle to vote, in accordance with the provisions of paragraphs 33 and 34 of these bylaws, that a meeting will be held at the time requested by the person or persons calling the meeting, not less than thirty-five (35) nor more than sixty (60) days after the receipt of the request. If the notice is not given within (20) days after receipt of the request, the Person or persons requesting the meeting may give the notice in the manner provided in these bylaws. Nothing contained in this paragraph shall be construed as limiting, fixing, or affecting the time when a meeting of shareholders called by action of the board of directors may be held.

33. Notice of meetings, annual or special, shall be given in writing not less than ten (10) nor more than sixty (60) days before the date of the meeting, to shareholders entitled to vote thereat by the Secretary or the Assistant Secretary, or if there be no such officer, or in the case of his or her neglect or refusal, by any director or shareholder. Such notices or any reports shall be given personally or by mail, or other means of communication as provided by state law, and shall be sent to the shareholder's address appearing on the books of the corporation, or supplied by him or her to the corporation for the purposes of notice. Notice of any meeting of shareholders shall

specify the place, date, and hour of the meeting and (i) in the case of a special meeting, the general nature of the business to be transacted, and no other business may be transacted, or (ii) in the case of an annual meeting, those matters which the board of directors, at the date of the mailing of notice, intends to present for action by the shareholders. At any meetings where directors are elected, notice shall include the names of the nominees, if any, intended at the date of notice to be presented by the management for election.

34. The presence in person or by proxy of the holders of a majority of the shares entitled to vote at any meeting of shareholders shall constitute a quorum for the transaction of business. The share-holders present at a duly called or held meeting at which a quorum is present may continue to do business until adjournment, notwithstanding the withdrawal of enough shareholders to leave less than a quorum, if any action taken (other than adjournment) is approved by at lease a majority of the shares required to constitute a quorum.

35. Any shareholders' meeting, annual or special, whether or not a quorum is present, may be adjourned from time to time by the vote of the majority of the shares represented at such meeting, either in person or by proxy, but in the absence of a quorum, no other business may be transacted at such meeting. When any meeting of shareholders, whether annual or special, is adjourned to another time or place, notice need not be given of the adjourned meeting if the time and place thereof are announced at a meeting at which the adjournment is taken, unless a new record date for the adjourned meting is fixed, or unless the adjournment is for more then forty-five (45) days from the date set for the original meeting, in which case the board of directors shall set a new record date. Notice of any such adjourned meeting shall be given to each shareholder of record entitled to vote at the adjourned meeting in accordance with the provisions of paragraph 33 of these bylaws.

36. The transactions at any meeting of shareholders, whether annual or special, however called and noticed, and wherever held, shall be as valid at though had at a meeting duly held after regular call and notice, if a quorum be present either in person or by proxy, signs a written waiver of notice or a consent to a holding of the meting, or any approval of the minutes thereof. All such waivers, consents, or approvals shall be filed with the corporate records or made a part of the minutes of the meeting.

37. A shareholder's attendance at a meting shall constitute a waiver of notice of such meeting, except when the shareholder objects at the beginning of the meeting.

38. Any action which may be taken at a meeting of the shareholders may be taken without a meting or notice of meeting if authorized by a writing signed by all of the shareholders entitled to vote at a meeting for such purpose and filed with the Secretary of the corporation.

39. Unless otherwise provided by state law, any action which may be taken at any annual or special meeting of shareholders may be taken without a meeting and without prior notice if a consent in writing setting for the action so taken shall be signed by the holders of outstanding shares having not less than the minimum number of votes that would be necessary to authorize or take such action at a meeting at which all shares entitled to vote thereon were present and voted.

40. Unless the consents of all shareholders entitled to vote have been solicited in writing, prompt notice shall be given of the taking of any other corporate action approved by shareholders without a meeting by less than unanimous written consent, to each of those shareholders entitled to vote who have not consented in writing.

41. Only persons in whose names shares entitled to vote stand on the stock records of the corporation on the day fixed by the board of directors for the determination of the shareholders of record, shall be entitled to vote at any shareholders' meeting. The board of directors may fix a time as a record date for the determination of the shareholders entitled to notice of and to vote at any such meeting, or entitled to receive any such dividend or distribution, or any allotment, rights, or to exercise the rights in respect to any such change, conversion, or exchange of shares. In such case only shareholders of record on the date so fixed shall be entitled to notice of and to vote at such meeting, or to receive such dividends, distribution, or allotment of rights or to exercise such rights, as the case may be, notwithstanding a transfer of any share on the books of the company after any record date fixed as aforesaid.

42. Every shareholder entitled to vote for directors or on any other matter shall have the right to do so either in person or by one or more agents authorized by a proxy validly executed by the shareholder. A proxy may be executed by written authorization signed, or by electronic transmission authorized, by the shareholder or the shareholder's attorney in fact, giving the proxy holder(s) the power to vote the shareholder's shares. A proxy shall be deemed signed if the shareholder's name or other authorization is placed on the proxy (whether by manual signature, typewriting, telegraphic or electronic transmission or otherwise) by the shareholder or the shareholder's attorney in fact. A proxy may also be transmitted orally by telephone if submitted with information from which it may be determined that

the proxy was authorized by the shareholder or the shareholder's attorney in fact. A validly executed proxy which does not state that it is irrevocable shall continue in full force and effect unless revoked by the person executing it, prior to the vote pursuant thereto, by a writing delivered to the corporation stating that the proxy is revoked or by a subsequent proxy executed by, or attendance at the meeting and voting in person by the person executing the proxy; provided, however, that no such proxy shall be valid after the expiration of (11) months from the date of such proxy, unless otherwise provided in the proxy.

43. The President, or in the absence of the President, any Vice President, shall call the meeting of the shareholders to order, and shall act as Chairman of the meeting. In the absence of the President and all the Vice Presidents, shareholders shall appoint a Chairman at such meeting. The Secretary of the Corporation shall act as Secretary of all meetings of the shareholders, but in the absence of the Secretary at any meeting of the shareholders, the presiding officer shall appoint any person to act as such Secretary of the meeting.

Part D. Shares

44. Certificates for shares shall be of such form and device as the board of directors may designate and shall state the name of the record holder of the shares represented thereby; its number and date of issuance; the number of shares for which it is issued; a statement of the rights, privileges, preferences, and restrictions, if any; a statement as to the redemption or conversion, if any; statement of liens or restrictions upon transfer or voting, if any; and if the shares be assessable, or if assessments are collectible by personal action, a plain statement of such facts.

45. Upon surrender to the Secretary or transfer agent of the corporation of a certificate for shares duly endorsed or accompanied by proper evidence of succession, assignment, or authority to transfer, it shall be the duty of the corporation to issue a new certificate to the person entitled thereto, cancel the old certificate, and record the transaction on its books.

46. In order that the corporation may determine the shareholders entitled to notice of any meeting or to vote, or entitled to receive payment of any dividend or other distribution or allotment of any rights or entitled to exercise any rights in respect of any lawful action, the board may fix in advance a record date, which shall not be more than

sixty (60) nor less than ten (10) days prior to the date of such meeting nor more than (60) days prior to any other action. If no record date is fixed:

(a) The record date for determining shareholders entitled to notice of or to vote at a meeting of shareholders shall be at the close of the business on the business day next preceding the day on which notice is given or, if notice is waived, at close of business on the business day next preceding the day on which the meeting is held.
(b) The record date for determining shareholders entitled to give consent to corporate action in writing without a meeting, when no prior action by the board is necessary, shall be the day on which the first written consent is given.
(c) The record date for determining shareholders for any other purpose shall be the close of business on the day on which the board adopts the resolution relating thereto, or the sixtieth (60th) day prior to the date of such other action, whichever is later.

Part E. Miscellaneous Matters

47. The corporation may at its option, to the maximum extent permitted by law and by the articles, indemnify each of its agents against expenses, judgments, fines, settlements, and other amounts actually and reasonably incurred in connection with any proceeding arising by reason of the fact that such person is or was an agent of the corporation. For the purposes of this section, an "agent" of the corporation, partnership, joint venture, trust, or other enterprise, or was a director, officer, employee, or agent of a corporation which was a predecessor corporation of the corporation or of any other enterprise at the request of such predecessor corporation.
48. The corporation shall keep at its principal executive office, or at the office of its transfer agent of registrar, if either be appointed and as determined by resolution of the board of directors, a record of its shareholders and the number and class of shares held by each shareholder.
49. The corporation shall keep at its principal executive office, or if its principal executive office is not in this state, at its principal business office in this state, the original or a copy of the bylaws amended to date, which shall be open to inspection by the shareholders at all reasonable times during office hours.

50. The board of directors, except as in the bylaws otherwise provide, may authorize any officer of officers, agent or agents, to enter into any contract or execute any instrument in the name of and on behalf of the corporation, and such authority may be general or confined to specific instances; and, unless so authorized or ratified by the board of directors or within the agency power of any officer, no officer, agent, or employee shall have any power or authority to bind the corporation by any contract or engagement or to pledge its credit or to render it liable for any purpose or to any amount.

51. The Chairman of the board, the President, or any Vice President, or any other person authorized by resolution of the board of directors by any of the foregoing designated officers, is authorized to vote on behalf of the corporation any and all shares of any other corporation or corporations, foreign or domestic, standing in the name of the corporation, The authority herein granted to side officers to vote or represent on behalf of the corporation any and all shares held by the corporation in any other corporation or corporation, may be exercised by any such officer in person or by any person authorized to do so by proxy duly elected by said officer.

52. These bylaws may be amended or replaced by the vote or written consent of the holders of a majority of the outstanding shares entitled to vote; provided, however, that if the Articles of Incorporation of the corporation set forth the number of authorized directors of the corporation, the authorized number of directors may be changed only by an amendment of the Articles of Incorporation. Bylaws may be adopted, amended, or repealed by the board of directors.

CERTIFICATE

I, (name), hereby certify that I am the Secretary of the initial meeting of [insert corporate name].

The foregoing bylaws, consisting of _____ pages, are a true and correct copy of the bylaws of the corporation.

IN WITNESS WHEREOF, I have hereunto set my hand and affixed the seal of the corporation this _____ day of _____, 20__

_____
[NAME OF SECRETARY]

I TRULY HOPE YOU ENJOYED AND USE THIS BOOK AND ROADMAP. GOOD LUCK IN ALL YOU DO.

References:

1. Financial Planning Tips
httpwww.macpa.orgcontentPublicDocumentsPDFbrochure.pdf
Accessed 5/18/10

2. Busop1.com
http://www.busop1.com/finplan.html
Accessed: 5/18/10

3. GetOutOfDebt.org
http://getoutofdebt.org/5270/one-way-to-protect-your-assets-from-creditors-in-case-you-might-get-sued
Accessed 5/16/10

4. Gimmelaw.com
http://www.gimmelaw.com/asset-protection-with-a-friendly-lien
Accessed: 5/16/10

5. Findlaw
http://smallbusiness.findlaw.com/business-structures/corporations/incorporate-pro-con.html
http://smallbusiness.findlaw.com/business-structures/corporations/corporations-s-corp-facts.html
Accessed Sunday 5/16/10

6. The Company Corporation
http://www.incorporate.com/benefits_of_incorporating.html
Accessed: 5/16/10

7. Entrepreneur Magazine's Guide To Forming Corporations, LLC's, Partnerships, Sole Proprietorships

8. Harvard Business Services Website

9. NOLO Learn About Law Series

TO PURCHASE COPIES OF THIS BOOK AND OR COPIES OF THE
"COMMERCIAL LENDERS DIRECTORY" OR "CREDIT SOLUTIONS"
PLEASE VISIT: www.businessbuilders.itgo.com

Appendix A

Excel Spreadsheets Containing Corporate Credit Use and Investment Returns.

Note: All Results Will Vary. The Larger Amount of Credit Use WILL Require More Investment To Establish The Initial Corporation Package. Also your choices of professional services to use and the variations in the stock market returns and your investment decision WILL result in variations. These charts are intended to only be indicative of what is possible not what is definite. No claims are made here as to what will happen only the possibility.

Be Sure You Are Familiarized With SEC Rules and IRS Rules Regarding Investment Companies So You Are BEST Educated As To The Rules Governing Your Activities And Responsibilities.

All of these Excel Spreadsheets are based upon the amount of Corporate Credit that can be obtained through Aged-Corporations.com, however the beginning corporate credit is obtained through The Company Corporation. Reference and contact information is available here in this book.

All Information Based On 2010 Facts and Figures

Tax Preparation (H&R/Yr)	80.00
Accounting (Quickbooks or Peachtree)	500.00
Attorney (Simplicitylaw.com basic ?'s)	100.00
Physical Address Service (www.delawareintercorp.com [99/Yr. Other 300/Yr.]	99.00
Phone Service (Skype VM free or Answer Connect ?50/Yr)	50.00
D&B (Self-Monitor/Yr)	550.00
Experian	99.00
Bank Accounts (@2 200/Chase 400/Other Once	400.00
State Fees (Delaware/Yr Min w/o Taxes)…	154.00
Portfolio Advising (Cramer Charitable…www.jim-cramer-charitable-trust-stocks.com)	0.00
Bank Requirements Certified Copies of State Filings Once	52.00
Registered Agent (DE Harvard Business Service / Companies Inc.)	50.00
3 Year Aged Corporation	3000.00
Tier 1 Credit (Companies Incorporated If You DIY All Other Stuff DNB etc.)	1600.00
Year 1 Startup Expense	6734.00

Tax Preparation (H&R/Yr) DIY Software	80.00
Accounting (Quickbooks or Peachtree)	500.00
Attorney (Simplicitylaw.com basic ?'s)	100.00
Physical Address Service (www.delawareintercorp.com [99/Yr. Other 300/Yr.]	99.00
Phone Service (Skype VM free or Answer Connect ?50/Yr)	50.00
D&B (Self-Monitor/Yr)	550.00
Experian	99.00
State Fees (Delaware/Yr Min w/o Taxes)…	154.00
Registered Agent (DE Harvard Business Service / Companies Inc.)	50.00
Annual Expenses At Lowest Rates Available	1682.00

YEAR 1

Credit: 250K	250000.00
Startup Expenses (Above)	6734.00
Credit To Be Used: 20% of Total Available	50000.00
40% Return Available or Better From Over 200 Mutual Funds Portfolio	20000.00
Tax Rate This Return (IRS): < 50,000 = 15%; Tax Is	3000.00
1st Year Interest Accrual Assume 15% All Years	7500.00

1st Year Returns After Tax and Interest Accrual	9500.00
1st Year Returns Less Startup Expenses	2766.00
1st Year Debt Service	2766.00

YEAR 2

Credit Used Including 1st Year Returns	47234.00
40% Return of Portfolio	20000.00
Tax Rate This Return (IRS): <50,000 = 15%; Tax Is	3000.00
2nd Year Interest Accrual Assume 15%	7085.10
2nd Year Annual Expenses	1682.00
2nd Year Returns Less Annual Expenses, Tax, and Interest Accrual	8232.90
2nd Year Debt Service	8232.90

YEAR 3

Credit Used Including 2nd Year Returns	39001.10
40% Return of Portfolio	20000.00
Tax Rate This Return (IRS): <50,000 = 15%; Tax Is	3000.00
3rd Year Interest Accrual Assume 15%	5850.17
3rd Year Annual Expenses	1682.00
3rd Year Returns Less Annual Expenses, Tax, and Interest Accrual	9467.84
3rd Year Debt Service	9467.84

YEAR 4

Credit Used Including 3rd Year Returns	29533.27
40% Return of Portfolio	20000.00
Tax Rate This Return (IRS): <50,000 = 15%; Tax Is	3000.00
4th Year Interest Accrual Assume 15%	4429.99
4th Year Annual Expenses	1682.00
4th Year Returns Less Annual Expenses, Tax, and Interest Accrual	10888.01
4th Year Debt Service	10888.01

YEAR 5

Credit Used Including 4th Year Returns	18645.25
40% Return of Portfolio	20000.00
Tax Rate This Return (IRS): <50,000 = 15%; Tax Is	3000.00
5th Year Interest Accrual Assume 15%	2796.79
5th Year Annual Expenses	1682.00
5th Year Returns Less Annual Expenses, Tax, and Interest Accrual	12521.21
5th Year Debt Service	12521.21

YEAR 6

Credit Used Including 5th Year Returns	6124.04
40% Return of Portfolio	20000.00
Tax Rate This Return (IRS): <50,000 = 15%; Tax Is	3000.00
6th Year Interest Accrual Assume 15%	918.61

6th Year Annual Expenses	1682.00
6th Year Returns Less Annual Expenses, Tax, and Interest Accrual	14399.39
6th Year Debt Service	14399.39

YEAR 7

Credit Used Including 6th Year Returns	0.00
6th Year Profit and Portfolio Reinvestment	8275.35
6th Year Portfolio Starting Amount	58275.35
6th Year Portfolio With Re-Use of 20%Available Credit (50,000)	108275.35
Credit Used Initial Again	50000.00
40% Rate of Return on Total Portfolio	43310.14
Tax Rate This Return (IRS): <50,000 = 15%; Tax Is	6496.52
7th Year Interest Accrual Assume 15% (of Credit Used)	7500.00
7th Year Annual Expenses	1682.00
7th Year Returns Less Annual Expenses, Tax, and Interest Accrual	27631.62
7th Year Debt Service	27631.62

YEAR 8

Credit Used Including 7th Year Returns	22368.38
40% Rate Of Return on Total Portfolio	43310.14
Tax Rate This Return (IRS): <50,000 = 15%; Tax Is	6496.52
8th Year Interest Accrual Assume 15%	3355.26
8th Year Annual Expenses	1682.00
8th Year Returns Less Annual Expenses, Tax, and Interest Accrual	31776.36
8th Year Debt Service	22368.38
8th Year Reinvestment Into Portfolio	9407.98

YEAR 9

Credit Used Again 50,000 Starting All Debt Service Paid Off In Year 8	50000.00
40% Rate Of Return into Total Portfolio (Y8+Y8Profit+50k Credit)	67073.33
Y9 Total Porfolio Value	167683.33
Tax Rate This Return 7,500 +25% of Amount over 50,000	11768.33
9th Year Interest Accrual Assume 15%	7500.00
9th Year Annual Expenses	1682.00
9th Year Returns Less Annual Expenses, Tax, and Interest Accrual	46123.00
9th Year Debt Service	46123.00

YEAR 10

Credit Used Including 9th Year Returns	3877.00
Y10 Portfolio Value	167683.33
40% Rate Of Return	67073.33
Tax Rate This Return 7,500 +25% of Amount over 50,000	11768.33
10th Year Interest Accrual Assume 15%	581.55
10th Year Annual Expenses	1682.00
10th Year Returns Less Annual Expenses, Tax, and Interest Accrual	53041.45

10th Year Debt Service	3877.00
10th Year Reinvestment Into Portfolio	49164.45

YEAR 11

Credit Used Again 50,000 Starting All Debt Service Paid Off in Year 10	50000.00
Y11 Portfolio Value	266847.78
40% Rate of Return	106739.11
Tax Rate This Return 22,250 + 39% of Amount over 100,000	24878.25
11th Year Interest Accrual Assume 15%	7500.00
11th Year Annual Expenses	1682.00
11th Year Returns Less Annual Expenses, Tax, and Interest Accrual	72678.86
11th Year Debt Service	50000.00
11th Year Reinvestment Into Portfolio	22678.86

YEAR 12

Credit Used Again 50,000 Starting All Debt Service Paid Off in Year 11	50000.00
Y12 Portfoio Value	339526.64
40% Rate of Return	135810.66
Tax Rate This Return 22,250 + 39% of Amount over 100,000	36216.16
12th Year Interest Accrual Assume 15%	7500.00
12th Year Annual Expenses	1682.00
12th Year Returns Less Annual Expenses, Tax, and Interest Accrual	90412.50
12th Year Debt Service	50000.00
12th Year Reinvestment Into Portfolio	40412.50

YEAR 13

Credit Used Again 50,000 Starting All Debt Service Paid Off in Year 12	50000.00
Y13 Portfolio Value	429939.14
40% Rate of Return	171975.66
Tax Rate This Return 22,250 + 39% of Amount over 100,000	50320.51
13th Year Interest Accrual Assume 15%	7500.00
13th Year Annual Expenses	1682.00
13th Year Returns Less Annual Expenses, Tax, and Interest Accrual	112473.15
13th Year Debt Service	50000.00
13th Year Reinvestment Into Portfolio	62473.15

YEAR 14

Credit Used Again 50,000 Starting All Debt Service Paid Off in Year 13	50000.00
Y14 Portfolio Value	542412.29
40% Rate of Return	216964.92
Tax Rate This Return 22,250 + 39% of Amount over 100,000	67866.32
14th Year Interest Accrual Assume 15%	7500.00
14th Year Annual Expenses	1682.00
14th Year Returns Less Annual Expenses, Tax, and Interest Accrual	139916.60
14th Year Debt Service	50000.00

14th Year Reinvestment Into Portfolio	89916.60

YEAR 15

Credit Used Again 50,000 Starting All Debt Service Paid Off In Year 14	50000.00
Y15Portfolio Value	682328.89
40% Rate of Return	272931.56
Tax Rate This Return 22,250 + 39% of Amount over 100,000	89693.31
15th Year Interest Accrual Assume 15%	7500.00
15th Year Annual Expenses	1682.00
15th Year Returns Less Annual Expenses, Tax, and Interest Accrual	174056.25
15th Year Debt Service	50000.00
15th Year Reinvestment Into Portfolio	124056.25

YEAR 16 Starting Portfolio Value with New 50000 Credit	856385.14

You Take It From There!!!

YEAR 1

Credit: 500K	500000.00
Startup Expenses (Above)	6734.00
Credit To Be Used: 20% of Total Available	100000.00
40% Return Available or Better From Over 200 Mutual Funds Portfolio	40000.00
Tax Rate This Return (IRS): < 50,000 = 15%; Tax Is	6000.00
1st Year Interest Accrual Assume 15% All Years	15000.00
1st Year Returns After Tax and Interest Accrual	19000.00
1st Year Returns Less Startup Expenses	12266.00
1st Year Debt Service	12266.00

YEAR 2

Credit Used Including 1st Year Returns	87734.00
40% Return of Portfolio	40000.00
Tax Rate This Return (IRS): <50,000 = 15%; Tax Is	6000.00
2nd Year Interest Accrual Assume 15%	13160.10
2nd Year Annual Expenses	1682.00
2nd Year Returns Less Annual Expenses, Tax, and Interest Accrual	19157.90
2nd Year Debt Service	19157.90

YEAR 3

Credit Used Including 2nd Year Returns	68576.10
40% Return of Portfolio	40000.00
Tax Rate This Return (IRS): <50,000 = 15%; Tax Is	6000.00
3rd Year Interest Accrual Assume 15%	10286.42

3rd Year Annual Expenses	1682.00
3rd Year Returns Less Annual Expenses, Tax, and Interest Accrual	22031.59
3rd Year Debt Service	22031.59

YEAR 4

Credit Used Including 3rd Year Returns	46544.52
40% Return of Portfolio	40000.00
Tax Rate This Return (IRS): <50,000 = 15%; Tax Is	6000.00
4th Year Interest Accrual Assume 15%	6981.68
4th Year Annual Expenses	1682.00
4th Year Returns Less Annual Expenses, Tax, and Interest Accrual	25336.32
4th Year Debt Service	25336.32

YEAR 5

Credit Used Including 4th Year Returns	21208.19
40% Return of Portfolio	40000.00
Tax Rate This Return (IRS): <50,000 = 15%; Tax Is	6000.00
5th Year Interest Accrual Assume 15%	3181.23
5th Year Annual Expenses	1682.00
5th Year Returns Less Annual Expenses, Tax, and Interest Accrual	29136.77
5th Year Debt Service	29136.77

YEAR 6

Credit Used Including 5th Year Returns	100000.00
Y6 Starting Portfolio	207928.58
40% Return of Portfolio	83171.43
Tax Rate This Return (IRS): 13,750 + 34% Amt Over 50,000	25028.29
6th Year Interest Accrual Assume 15%	15000.00
6th Year Annual Expenses	1682.00
6th Year Returns Less Annual Expenses, Tax, and Interest Accrual	41461.14
6th Year Debt Service	41461.14

YEAR 7

Credit Used	58538.86
Y7 Starting Portfolio	207928.58
40% Return of Portfolio	83171.43
Tax Rate This Return (IRS): 13,750 + 34% Amt Over 50,000	25028.29
7th Year Interest Accrual Assume 15%	8780.83
7th Year Annual Expenses	1682.00
7th Year Returns Less Annual Expenses, Tax, and Interest Accrual	47680.32

YEAR 8

Credit Reuse 20% Since Paid Off Y7	100000.00
Y8 Starting Portfolio	297070.04
40% Return of Portfolio	118828.02

Tax Rate This Return (IRS): 22,250 + 39% of Amt Over 100,000	29592.93
8th Year Interest Accrual Assume 15%	15000.00
8th Year Annual Expenses	1682.00
8th Year Returns Less Annual Expenses, Tax, and Interest Accrual	72553.09

YEAR 9

Credit Used	27446.91
Y9 Starting Portfolio	297070.04
40% Return of Portfolio	118828.02
Tax Rate This Return (IRS): 22,250 + 39% of Amt Over 100,000	29592.93
9th Year Interest Accrual Assume 15%	4117.04
9th Year Annual Expenses	1682.00
9th Year Returns Less Annual Expenses, Tax, and Interest Accrual	83436.05

YEAR 10

Credit Reuse 20% Since Paid Off Y9	100000.00
Y10 Starting Portfolio	453059.18
40% Return of Portfolio	181223.67
Tax Rate This Return (IRS): 22,250 + 39% of Amt Over 100,000	53927.23
10th Year Interest Accrual Assume 15%	15000.00
10th Year Annual Expenses	1682.00
10th Year Returns Less Annual Expenses, Tax, and Interest Accrual	110614.44

YEAR 11

Credit Reuse 20% Since Paid Off Y10	100000.00
Y11 Starting Portfolio	563673.62
40% Return of Portfolio	225469.45
Tax Rate This Return (IRS): 22,250 + 39% of Amt Over 100,000	71183.09
11th Year Interest Accrual Assume 15%	15000.00
11th Year Annual Expenses	1682.00
11th Year Returns Less Annual Expenses, Tax, and Interest Accrual	137604.36

YEAR 12

Credit Reuse 20% Since Paid Off Y11	100000.00
Y12 Starting Portfolio	701277.99
40% Return of Portfolio	280511.20
Tax Rate This Return (IRS): 22,250 + 39% of Amt Over 100,000	92649.37
12th Year Interest Accrual Assume 15%	15000.00
12th Year Annual Expenses	1682.00
12th Year Returns Less Annual Expenses, Tax, and Interest Accrual	171179.83

YEAR 13

Credit Reuse 20% Since Paid Off Y12	100000.00
Y13 Starting Portfolio	872457.82
40% Returns	348983.13

Tax Rate This Return (IRS): 113,900 + 34% of Amt Over 335,000	118654.26
13th Year Interest Accrual Assume 15%	15000.00
13th Year Annual Expenses	1682.00
13th Year Returns Less Annual Expenses, Tax, and Interest Accrual	213646.86

YEAR 14

Credit Reuse 20% Since Paid Off Y13	100000.00
Y14 Starting Portfolio	1086104.68
40% Returns	434441.87
Tax Rate This Return (IRS): 113,900 + 34% of Amt Over 335,000	147710.24
14th Year Interest Accrual Assume 15%	15000.00
14th Year Annual Expenses	1682.00
14th Year Returns Less Annual Expenses, Tax, and Interest Accrual	270049.64

YEAR 15

Credit Reuse 20% Since Paid Off Y14	100000.00
Y15 Starting Portfolio	1356154.32
40% Returns	542461.73
Tax Rate This Return (IRS): 113,900 + 34% of Amt Over 335,000	184436.99
15th Year Interest Accrual Assume 15%	15000.00
15th Year Annual Expenses	1682.00
15th Year Returns Less Annual Expenses, Tax, and Interest Accrual	357751.74

Y16

CR REUSE	100k
Y16 STRT PORTFOLIO	1713906.06
40% RTN	685562.42
YEAR 1	

YEAR 1

Credit: 1,000,000	1000000.00
Startup Expenses 6,734 + 65,000	71734.00
Credit To Be Used: 20% of Total Available	200000.00
40% Return Available or Better From Over 200 Mutual Funds Portfolio	80000.00
Tax Rate This Return (IRS): 13,750 +34% Amt Over 75,000	15450.00
1st Year Interest Accrual Assume 15% All Years	30000.00
1st Year Returns Less Startup Expenses	-37184.00
1st Year Debt Service	-37184.00

YEAR 2

Credit Used Including 1st Year Returns	237184.00

Y2 Portfolio	200000.00
40% Return of Portfolio	80000.00
Tax Rate This Return (IRS): 13,750 + 34% Amt Over 75000	15450.00
2nd Year Interest Accrual Assume 15%	35577.60
2nd Year Annual Expenses	1682.00
2nd Year Returns Less Annual Expenses, Tax, and Interest Accrual	27290.40
2nd Year Debt Service	27290.40

YEAR 3

Credit Used Including 2nd Year Returns	209893.60
Y3 Portfolio	200000.00
40% Return of Portfolio	80000.00
Tax Rate This Return (IRS): 13,750 + 34% Amt Over 75,000	15450.00
3rd Year Interest Accrual Assume 15%	31484.04
3rd Year Annual Expenses	1682.00
3rd Year Returns Less Annual Expenses, Tax, and Interest Accrual	31383.96
3rd Year Debt Service	31383.96

YEAR 4

Credit Used Including 3rd Year Returns	178509.64
Y4 Portfolio	200000.00
40% Return of Portfolio	80000.00
Tax Rate This Return (IRS): 13,750 + 34% Amt Over 75,000	15450.00
4th Year Interest Accrual Assume 15%	26776.45
4th Year Annual Expenses	1682.00
4th Year Returns Less Annual Expenses, Tax, and Interest Accrual	36091.55
4th Year Debt Service	36091.55

YEAR 5

Credit Used Including 4th Year Returns	142418.09
Y5 Portfolio	200000.00
40% Return of Portfolio	80000.00
Tax Rate This Return (IRS): 13,750 + 34% Amt Over 75,000	15450.00
5th Year Interest Accrual Assume 15%	21362.71
5th Year Annual Expenses	1682.00
5th Year Returns Less Annual Expenses, Tax, and Interest Accrual	41505.29
5th Year Debt Service	41505.29

YEAR 6

Credit Used	100912.80
Y6 Portfolio Amount	200000.00
40% Return of Portfolio	80000.00
Tax Rate This Return (IRS): 13,750 + 34% Amt Over 75,000	15450.00
6th Year Interest Accrual Assume 15%	15136.92
6th Year Annual Expenses	1682.00

6th Year Returns Less Annual Expenses, Tax, and Interest Accrual	47731.08
6th Year Debt Service	47731.08

YEAR 7

Credit Used	53181.72
Y7 Portfolio Amount	200000.00
40% Returns	80000.00
Tax Rate This Return (IRS): 13,750 + 34% Amt Over 75,000	15450.00
7th Year Interest Accrual Assume 15%	7977.26
7th Year Annual Expenses	1682.00
7th Year Returns Less Annual Expenses, Tax, and Interest Accrual	54890.74
7th Year Profit/Reinvest	1709.02

YEAR 8

Credit Reused	200000.00
Y8 Portfolio Amount	401709.02
40% Returns	160683.61
Tax Rate This Return (IRS): 22,250 + 39% Amt Over 100,000	45916.61
8th Year Interest Accrual Assume 15%	30000.00
8th Year Annual Expenses	1682.00
8th Year Returns Less Annual Expenses, Tax, and Interest Accrual	83085.00
8th Year Debt Service	116915.00

YEAR 9

Credit Used	83085.00
Y9 Portfolio Amount	401709.02
40% Returns	160683.61
Tax Rate This Return (IRS): 22,250 + 39% Amt Over 100,000	45916.61
9th Year Interest Accrual Assume 15%	12462.75
9th Year Annual Expenses	1682.00
9th Year Returns Less Annual Expenses, Tax, and Interest Accrual	100622.25
9th Year Profit/Reinvest	17537.25

YEAR 10

Credit Reused	200000.00
Y10 Portfolio Amount	619246.27
40% Returns	247698.51
Tax Rate This Return (IRS): 22,250 + 39% Amt Over 100,000	79852.42
10th Year Interest Accrual Assume 15%	30000.00
10th Year Annual Expenses	1682.00
10th Year Returns Less Annual Expenses, Tax, and Interest Accrual	136164.09
10th Year Debt Service	136164.09

YEAR 11

Credit Used	63835.91

Y11 Portfolio Value	619246.27
40% Returns	247698.51
Tax Rate This Return (IRS): 22,250 + 39% Amt Over 100,000	79852.42
11th Year Interest Accrual Assume 15%	9575.39
11th Year Annual Expenses	1682.00
11th Year Returns Less Annual Expenses, Tax, and Interest Accrual	156588.70
11th Year Profit/Reinvestment	92752.79

YEAR 12

Credit Reused	200000.00
Y12 Portfoio Value	911999.07
40% Rate of Return	364799.63
Tax Rate This Return (IRS): 113,900 + 34% Amt Over 335,000	124031.87
12th Year Interest Accrual Assume 15%	30000.00
12th Year Annual Expenses	1682.00
12th Year Returns Less Annual Expenses, Tax, and Interest Accrual	209085.75
12th Year Profit/Reinvest	9085.75

YEAR 13

Credit Reused	200000.00
Y13 Portfolio Value	1121084.82
40% Returns	448433.93
Tax Rate This Return (IRS): 113,900 + 34% Amt Over 335,000	152467.54
13th Year Interest Accrual Assume 15%	30000.00
13th Year Annual Expenses	1682.00
13th Year Returns Less Annual Expenses, Tax, and Interest Accrual	264284.39
13th Year Profit/Reinvest	64284.39

YEAR 14

Credit Reused	200000.00
Y14 Portfolio Value	1385369.22
40% Returns	554147.69
Tax Rate This Return (IRS): 113,900 + 34% Amt Over 335,000	188410.21
14th Year Interest Accrual Assume 15%	30000.00
14th Year Annual Expenses	1682.00
14th Year Returns Less Annual Expenses, Tax, and Interest Accrual	334055.47
14th Year Profit/Reinvest	134055.47

YEAR 15

Credit Reused	200000.00
Y15 Portfolio Value	1719424.69
40% Rate of Return	687769.88
Tax Rate This Return (IRS): 113,900 + 34% Amt Over 335,000	233841.76
15th Year Interest Accrual Assume 15%	30000.00
15th Year Annual Expenses	1682.00

15th Year Returns Less Annual Expenses, Tax, and Interest Accrual	422246.12
15th Year Profit/Reinvest	222246.12
YEAR 16 Starting Portfolio Value with New 50000 Credit	2141670.81
You Take It From There!!!	

YEAR 1

Credit: 2500000	2500000.00
Startup Expenses 6,734+ 95,000	101734.00
Credit To Be Used: 20% of Total Available	500000.00
40% Return Available or Better From Over 200 Mutual Funds	
Portfolio	200000.00
Tax Rate This Return (IRS): 22,250 + 39% Amt Over 100,000	61250.00
1st Year Interest Accrual Assume 15%	75000.00
1st Year Returns After Annual Expenses, Tax, and Accrued Interest	-37984.00
1st Year Debt Service	-37984.00

YEAR 2
Credit Used	537984.00
Y2 Portfolio	500000.00
40% Returns	200000.00
Tax Rate This Return (IRS): 22,250 + 39% Amt Over 100000	61250.00
2nd Year Interest Accrual Assume 15%	80697.60
2nd Year Annual Expenses	1682.00
2nd Year Returns Less Annual Expenses, Tax, and Interest Accrual	56370.40
2nd Year Debt Service	56370.40

YEAR 3
Credit Used	481613.60
Y3 Portfolio	500000.00
40% Returns	200000.00
Tax Rate This Return (IRS): 22,250 + 39% Amt Over 100,000	61250.00
3rd Year Interest Accrual Assume 15%	72242.04
3rd Year Annual Expenses	1682.00
3rd Year Returns Less Annual Expenses, Tax, and Interest Accrual	64825.96
3rd Year Debt Service	64825.96

YEAR 4
Credit Used	416787.64
Y4 Portfolio	500000.00
40% Return of Portfolio	200000.00

Tax Rate This Return (IRS): 22,250 + 39% Amt Over 100000	61250.00
4th Year Interest Accrual Assume 15%	62518.15
4th Year Annual Expenses	1682.00
4th Year Returns Less Annual Expenses, Tax, and Interest Accrual	74549.85
4th Year Debt Service	74549.85

YEAR 5

Credit Used	342237.79
Y5 Portfolio	500000.00
40% Return of Portfolio	200000.00
Tax Rate This Return (IRS): 22,250 + 39% Amt Over 100,000	61250.00
5th Year Interest Accrual Assume 15%	51335.67
5th Year Annual Expenses	1682.00
5th Year Returns Less Annual Expenses, Tax, and Interest Accrual	85732.33
5th Year Debt Service	85732.33

YEAR 6

Credit Used	256505.45
Y6 Portfolio	500000.00
40% Returns	200000.00
Tax Rate This Return (IRS): 22,250 + 39% Amt Over 100,000	61250.00
6th Year Interest Accrual Assume 15%	38475.82
6th Year Annual Expenses	1682.00
6th Year Returns Less Annual Expenses, Tax, and Interest Accrual	98592.18
6th Year Debt Service and Profit/Reinvest	98592.18

YEAR 7

Credit Used	157913.27
Y7 Portfolio	500000.00
40% Returns	200000.00
Tax Rate This Return (IRS): 22,250 + 39% Amt Over 100,000	61250.00
7th Year Interest Accrual Assume 15%	23686.99
7th Year Annual Expenses	1682.00
7th Year Returns Less Annual Expenses, Tax, and Interest Accrual	113381.01
7th Year Debt Service and Profit/Reinvest	113381.01

YEAR 8

Credit Used	44532.26
Y8 Portfolio	500000.00
40% Returns	200000.00
Tax Rate This Return (IRS): 22,250 + 39% Amt Over 100,000	61250.00
8th Year Interest Accrual Assume 15%	6679.84
8th Year Annual Expenses	1682.00
8th Year Returns Less Annual Expenses, Tax, and Interest Accrual	130388.16
8th Year Profit/Reinvest	85855.90

YEAR 9

Credit Reused	500000.00
Y9 Portfolio	1085855.90
40% Returns	434342.36
Tax Rate This Return (IRS): 113,900 + 34% Amt Over 335,000	147676.40
9th Year Interest Accrual Assume 15%	75000.00
9th Year Annual Expenses	1682.00
9th Year Returns Less Annual Expenses, Tax, and Interest Accrual	209983.96
9th Year Debt Service	209983.96

YEAR 10

Credit Used	290016.04
Y10 Portfolio	1085855.90
40% Rate Of Return	434342.36
Tax Rate This Return (IRS): 113,900 + 34% Amt Over 335,000	147676.40
10th Year Interest Accrual Assume 15%	43502.41
10th Year Annual Expenses	1682.00
10th Year Returns Less Annual Expenses, Tax, and Interest Accrual	241481.55
10th Year Debt Service and Profit/Reinvest	241481.55

YEAR 11

Credit Used	48534.49
Y11 Portfolio	1085855.90
40% Rate of Return	434342.36
Tax Rate This Return (IRS): 113,900 + 34% Amt Over 335,000	147676.40
11th Year Interest Accrual Assume 15%	7280.17
11th Year Annual Expenses	1682.00
11th Year Returns Less Annual Expenses, Tax, and Interest Accrual	277703.78
11th Year Profit/Reinvest	229169.29

YEAR 12

Credit Reused	500000.00
Y12 Portfoio	1815025.19
40% Rate of Return	726010.08
Tax Rate This Return (IRS): 113,900 + 34% Amt Over 335,000	246843.43
12th Year Interest Accrual Assume 15%	75000.00
12th Year Annual Expenses	1682.00
12th Year Returns Less Annual Expenses, Tax, and Interest Accrual	402484.65
12th Year Debt Service and Profit/Reinvest	402484.65

YEAR 13

Credit Used	97515.35
Y13 Portfolio	1815025.19
40% Returns	726010.08
Tax Rate This Return (IRS): 113,900 + 34% Amt Over 335000	246843.43
13th Year Interest Accrual Assume 15%	14627.30
13th Year Annual Expenses	1682.00
13th Year Returns Less Annual Expenses, Tax, and Interest Accrual	462857.35
13th Year Profit/Reinvest	365342.00
YEAR 14	
Credit Reused	500000.00
Y14 Portfolio	2680367.19
40% Returns	1072146.87
Tax Rate This Return (IRS): 113,900 + 34% Amt Over 335,000	364529.94
14th Year Interest Accrual Assume 15%	75000.00
14th Year Annual Expenses	1682.00
14th Year Returns Less Annual Expenses, Tax, and Interest Accrual	630934.94
14th Year Profit/Reinvest	130934.94
YEAR 15	
Credit Reused	500000.00
Y15 Portfolio	3311302.12
40% Returns	1324520.85
Tax Rate This Return (IRS): 113,900 + 34% Amt Over 335000	450337.09
15th Year Interest Accrual Assume 15%	75000.00
15th Year Annual Expenses	1682.00
15th Year Returns Less Annual Expenses, Tax, and Interest Accrual	797501.76
15th Year Profit/Reinvest	297501.76
YEAR 16 Starting Portfolio Value with New 500000 Credit ReUse You Take It From There!!!	4311302.12

YEAR 1	
Credit: 5000000	5000000.00
Startup Expenses 6,734 + 180,000	186734.00
Credit To Be Used: 20% of Total Available	1000000.00
40% Return Available or Better From Over 200 Mutual Funds Portfolio	400000.00
Tax Rate This Return (IRS): 113,900 + 34% Amt Over 335,000	136000.00

1st Year Interest Accrual Assume 15%	150000.00
1st Year Returns After Annual Expenses, Tax, and Accrued Interest	-72734.00
1st Year Debt Service	-72734.00

YEAR 2

Credit Used	1072734.00
Y2 Portfolio	1000000.00
40% Returns	400000.00
Tax Rate This Return (IRS): 113,900 + 34% Amt Over 335,000	136000.00
2nd Year Interest Accrual Assume 15%	160910.10
2nd Year Annual Expenses	1682.00
2nd Year Returns Less Annual Expenses, Tax, and Interest Accrual	101407.90
2nd Year Debt Service	101407.90

YEAR 3

Credit Used	971326.10
Y3 Portfolio	1000000.00
40% Returns	400000.00
Tax Rate This Return (IRS): 113,900 + 34% Amt Over 335,000	136000.00
3rd Year Interest Accrual Assume 15%	145698.92
3rd Year Annual Expenses	1682.00
3rd Year Returns Less Annual Expenses, Tax, and Interest Accrual	116619.09
3rd Year Debt Service	116619.09

YEAR 4

Credit Used	854707.02
Y4 Portfolio	1000000.00
40% Return of Portfolio	400000.00
Tax Rate This Return (IRS): 113,900 + 34% Amt Over 335,000	136000.00
4th Year Interest Accrual Assume 15%	128206.05
4th Year Annual Expenses	1682.00
4th Year Returns Less Annual Expenses, Tax, and Interest Accrual	134111.95
4th Year Debt Service	134111.95

YEAR 5

Credit Used	720595.07
Y5 Portfolio	1000000.00
40% Return of Portfolio	400000.00
Tax Rate This Return (IRS): 113,900 + 34% Amt Over 335,000	136000.00
5th Year Interest Accrual Assume 15%	108089.26
5th Year Annual Expenses	1682.00
5th Year Returns Less Annual Expenses, Tax, and Interest Accrual	154228.74
5th Year Debt Service	154228.74

YEAR 6

Credit Used	566366.33
Y6 Portfolio	1000000.00
40% Returns	400000.00
Tax Rate This Return (IRS): 113,900 + 34% Amt Over 335,000	136000.00
6th Year Interest Accrual Assume 15%	84954.95
6th Year Annual Expenses	1682.00
6th Year Returns Less Annual Expenses, Tax, and Interest Accrual	177363.05
6th Year Debt Service	177363.05

YEAR 7

Credit Used	389003.28
Y7 Portfolio	1000000.00
40% Returns	400000.00
Tax Rate This Return (IRS): 113,900 + 34% Amt Over 335,000	136000.00
7th Year Interest Accrual Assume 15%	58350.49
7th Year Annual Expenses	1682.00
7th Year Returns Less Annual Expenses, Tax, and Interest Accrual	203967.51
7th Year Debt Service	203967.51

YEAR 8

Credit Used	185035.77
Y8 Portfolio	1000000.00
40% Returns	400000.00
Tax Rate This Return (IRS): 113,900 + 34% Amt Over 335,000	136000.00
8th Year Interest Accrual Assume 15%	27755.37
8th Year Annual Expenses	1682.00
8th Year Returns Less Annual Expenses, Tax, and Interest Accrual	234562.63
8th Year Profit/Reinvest	49526.87

YEAR 9

Credit Reused	1000000.00
Y9 Portfolio	2049526.87
40% Returns	819810.75
Tax Rate This Return (IRS): 113,900 + 34% Amt Over 335,000	278735.65
9th Year Interest Accrual Assume 15%	150000.00
9th Year Annual Expenses	1682.00
9th Year Returns Less Annual Expenses, Tax, and Interest Accrual	389393.09
9th Year Debt Service	389393.09

YEAR 10

Credit Used	610606.91
Y10 Portfolio	2049526.87
40% Rate Of Return	819810.75
Tax Rate This Return (IRS): A36	278735.65
10th Year Interest Accrual Assume 15%	91591.04

10th Year Annual Expenses	1682.00
10th Year Returns Less Annual Expenses, Tax, and Interest Accrual	447802.06
10th Year Debt Service	447802.06

YEAR 11

Credit Used	162804.85
Y11 Portfolio	2049526.87
40% Rate of Return	819810.75
Tax Rate This Return (IRS): 113,900 + 34% Amt Over 335,000	278735.65
11th Year Interest Accrual Assume 15%	24420.73
11th Year Annual Expenses	1682.00
11th Year Returns Less Annual Expenses, Tax, and Interest Accrual	514972.37
11th Year Profit/Reinvest	352167.51

YEAR 12

Credit Reused	1000000.00
Y12 Portfoio	3401694.38
40% Rate of Return	1360677.75
Tax Rate This Return (IRS): 113,900 + 34% Amt Over 335,000	462630.44
12th Year Interest Accrual Assume 15%	150000.00
12th Year Annual Expenses	1682.00
12th Year Returns Less Annual Expenses, Tax, and Interest Accrual	746365.32
12th Year Debt Service	746365.32

YEAR 13

Credit Used	253634.68
Y13 Portfolio	3401694.38
40% Returns	1360677.75
Tax Rate This Return (IRS): 113,900 + 34% Amt Over 335000	462630.44
13th Year Interest Accrual Assume 15%	38045.20
13th Year Annual Expenses	1682.00
13th Year Returns Less Annual Expenses, Tax, and Interest Accrual	858320.11
13th Year Profit/Reinvest	604685.43

YEAR 14

Credit Reused	1000000.00
Y14 Portfolio	5006379.81
40% Returns	2002551.93
Tax Rate This Return (IRS): 113,900 + 34% Amt Over 335,000	680867.65
14th Year Interest Accrual Assume 15%	150000.00
14th Year Annual Expenses	1682.00

14th Year Returns Less Annual Expenses, Tax, and Interest
Accrual   1170002.27
14th Year Profit/Reinvest   1170002.27

YEAR 15
Credit Reused   1000000.00
Y15 Portfolio   7176382.08
40% Returns   2870552.83
Tax Rate This Return (IRS): 113,900 + 34% Amt Over 335000   975987.96
15th Year Interest Accrual Assume 15%   150000.00
15th Year Annual Expenses   1682.00
15th Year Returns Less Annual Expenses, Tax, and Interest
Accrual   1742882.87
15th Year Profit/Reinvest   742882.87

YEAR 16 Starting Portfolio Value with New 1000000   8919264.95
You Take It From There!!!

_____

Signing up with Morninstar.com and using the Fund Screener is the way to
find the Top Performing Funds for the last year. Their results of
performance are in no way indicative of the next year best performing funds.